GOD
Help Me Find

Daily Devotionals for Inspired Living

Robert Moment

LEGAL STATEMENT

Help Me Find God

ISBN-13: 978-0-9799982-8-7

LIABILITY/WARRANTY

Table of Contents

HE LEADTH ME

Heavenly Father,

Thanks for loving me just as I am. I choose to recognize my worth in You.

Thank You for being with me, right now.

I seek Your face. Help me to draw closer to You. Transform my life by Your Spirit.

Give me a personal encounter with You.

Speak to me. Teach me. Change me. Guide me.

I trust You.

Thank You for being my constant companion and guide.

In Jesus Name. Amen

INTRODUCTION

"Belonging to and believing in God brings boundless blessings in our lives"
— *Robert Moment*

Take an honest look at your life. Do you feel something is missing in your life? Are you searching for love, peace and happiness? Right now, how do you feel about your life? What do you want out of life? Do you want to feel whole and complete?

Why are you reading this? What has brought you to this point? Perhaps you're curious to learn more of this enigmatic, all powerful God that people talk about.

Perhaps you just wondered what all the fuss was about.

Some of you may be battling with a difficult time in your life and wondering how to cope. Perhaps, like so many of us, you sense a yearning deep inside of you, a gap which you can't identify, a need to be spiritually fulfilled yet you are struggling to know how to start.

What if you were offered an answer to that yearning?

What if someone said to you, I love you eternally, I love you unconditionally, I want you to fulfill your potential, I want what's best for you?

What if all of your sins were forgiven, wiped out in a single moment of grace?

What if there was a way to bring joy to your life no matter what circumstances you found yourself in?

What if someone promised you an inner peace beyond words?

What if the end of your earthly life wasn't the end and the promise of eternal life awaited you?

God's amazing promises give us all of that and more. There is a deep yearning at the core of all of us; the feeling that there is more to life than what we see, that the universe has so much more to offer than we can fully comprehend.

You may be familiar with the phrase a 'God shaped vacuum' which gives this yearning definition. It can best be described as a tangible yet inexplicable desire for our souls to find a fulfillment which only God can provide. Unfortunately, our materialistic world lacks the means and often the understanding to direct us towards the source of our fulfillment.

In the second century the priest Irenaeus described the glory of God as 'a human being fully alive'.

God's glorious promise of being fully alive is available to all of us. All we have to do is reach out to transform our lives and find the inner peace we all so badly crave.

You cannot know yourself by yourself.

A *connection* to God is the key to our fulfillment.

Chapter 1
FINDING A CLEAR PATH TO GOD

You've worked hard. You've done what has been asked of you. You've jumped through all the necessary hoops and accomplished your important goals—and yet, you still feel that you might be missing something in your life.

Each of us has a hole inside of us that longs to be filled by the One who created us. Many of us try to fill this hole with other things: romance, money, kids, hobbies, careers—but nothing ultimately satisfies. And the crazy thing is—these things that we think will make us happy sometimes get in the way of what will really make us happy: **God.**

In order to really discover who we are meant to be, we must clear a path for the One who created us. We must clear the path for God, and if this means moving some of the other "stuff" out of the way, then this is what we need to do.

We can spend our whole lives searching for something to fill the gap, or we can spend our lives seeking out the God that we know is there.

When you're new to this process, it can seem daunting. Maybe you're not even sure that you believe in God, yet you feel something or someone calling you to find out for sure. You are not alone. Millions of others have gone through this process before you, and have come out on the other end happy and fulfilled.

Don't be scared of religion. Don't let anger with religion come between you and your Creator. God is not about religion—He's about relationship, and He created you to have a personal relationship with Him.

So try to clear a path for Him, and just see what happens. Try to make some time for Him each day. Read a few Bible verses. The Bible is the Christians blueprint for living. Listen to some worship music. Pray. Just talk to God. Or just spend some quiet time alone with Him and listen for His voice.

You have worked hard. You have done what you were supposed to do. Now it's time to focus on what will really *complete* you, and what will really bring you *peace*. Now it's time to open your life to the life force, clear the path, and open the doors of your heart. You won't be sorry. Your life will finally make sense when you understand that you were *made by God* and *made for God*.

Seek God and develop a relationship with Him .

Call on God right now. He's waiting for You !

WHO IS GOD?

God is love (1 John 4:16).

The love of God prompted Him to create humans in His own image to share that love with us. He created each and every one of us. He has a purpose and a plan for our lives which was mapped out for us before we were born. God is outside our normal comprehension of what we call time. He is in our future, in our past and in our present.

In God's eyes we are all equal and we all have potential. He loves us all with a love we can barely begin to understand.

God made each human being with a spiritual potential. The more we become aware of ourselves in a sensitive and understanding way, the more we shall become aware of and understand God, becoming what He meant us to be, loving God and loving our neighbor.

God is eternal, truthful, faithful, merciful and just. He is omniscient and all-knowing. He is omnipresent. God is unchangeable. In other words, He does not change any of His attributes or character at any time.

Despite humanity's tendency to change its definition of morality, God's moral character does not evolve with the times, but remains constant.

He is our Creator, our Father and our Redeemer. He loves us, he wants what's best for us and he seeks a relationship with all of us. This relationship is open to each and everyone of us through faith in His son Jesus Christ.

While human life on earth is short, with Jesus life is eternal. Believing in Jesus fills our lives with joyful anticipation of our ultimate destination.

God is the ultimate, perfect in power, love, and character. He wants us to love him and love other people. God came to earth in human form as Jesus to teach us about himself and to provide the ultimate sacrifice for our sins, so that those who believe in Him can enjoy the blessings of His grace.

To benefit from God's love and promises, you have only to reach out to His son, our savior Jesus Christ.

GOD'S AMAZING PROMISES

Let's take a look at God's Amazing Promises for our lives. God rewards those who believe and obey His Word. Seek to be faithful to Him and experience His promises. Remember to Trust in Him and in Him alone. Be willing to believe that His Word is *true*. He *always* keeps His promises.

God will never leave us

Have I not commanded you? Be strong and courageous. Do not be afraid; do not be discouraged, for the Lord your God will be with you wherever you go (Joshua 1:9)

All of us hit low points in our lives where we struggle as we walk through the darkness, facing seemingly hopeless situations. With God in our lives, we don't have to be afraid. No matter how great the challenges, He is with us. In every situation in our lives we have the promise of God's protection. We are His children. Sometimes we're trapped in what seem like ever decreasing circles so we begin to expect the worst. Give yourself permission to believe God's promise of always being with us. Offer your life to Him and allow Him to do the rest.

We do not need to be afraid

Trust in the Lord with all your heart and lean not on your own understanding (Proverbs 3:5).

The Bible tells us over 100 times not to be afraid but it isn't always that easy. Our lives are full of problems. We fear for our children, our family, our jobs, our financial future and our health. God is with us in everything, there's no need to be afraid. Becoming a Christian doesn't mean our life will be instantly easy but it means God will be with us through all of our troubles and woes.

He has promised to fulfill our needs
And my God will meet all your needs according to the riches of his glory in Christ Jesus (Philippians 4:19).

The needs referred to here aren't those of a materialistic generation. God will fulfill our needs according to His plans and His purpose for us, He wants and knows what is best for us, although at times it doesn't always seem to correspond with what we think we need. When we trust God and walk towards Him in faith, we find we are equipped with everything we need to fulfill our purpose.

God has plans and a purpose for our lives
For I know the plans I have for you, declares the Lord, plans to prosper you and not to harm you, plans to give you hope and a future. Then you will call on me and come and pray to me, and I will listen to you. You will seek me and find me when you seek me with all your heart. (Jeremiah 29:11-13).

God has a plan for all of our lives, a plan to help us to find our true potential if we will only allow Him. Do as He says, trust him, call on him and seek him with all of your heart. He promises that you will find him.

God promises us peace

The peace of God, which transcends all understanding, will guard your hearts and your minds in Christ Jesus (Philippians 4:7)

The peace of God is an abiding peace that suffuses our hearts. Words cannot describe the joy we gain from that peace, from the certainty that God loves us and He is with us always. It is a peace that grants us a rare serenity.

He has promised us eternal life through His son, Jesus Christ.

For God so loved the world that he gave his one and only Son, that whoever believes in him shall not perish but have eternal life (John 3:16).

What an incredible promise. God so loved the world that he gave his son for us. When we have faith in Jesus Christ, we are promised the glory of an eternal life in God's Kingdom. An eternal life free from sorrow, pain and mourning

How do we receive God's promises? By turning to His son, our Savior, Jesus Christ.

WHAT JESUS CAN DO FOR YOU

Jesus is God's promise, His gift to the world, sent to save the world from itself. He is our Savior, our Redeemer and the Son of God. He is also referred to as Emmanuel, which literally means God with us.

Jesus is the Word of God made flesh. He didn't just tell people about God's compassion and mercy, of His holiness and power. He revealed and consequently taught those truths through His own life and ultimately, His death and resurrection. In doing so He lived among us to fully understand our experiences and temptations, to live a human life in all its fragility.

Yet He was without sin and died on the cross to take upon himself the sins of the world so we might again be able to draw closer to God through Him. Our hope lies in His resurrection and defeat of death that we might have eternal life.

Through Jesus, we can find peace, fulfillment, self-worth, provision, contentment , security, protection, guidance and so many other assurances we seek in life.

How amazing are those promises.

A life in Christ means He is with us every day through His Holy Spirit.

This is Jesus in his own words:-

"I am the light of the world
he who follows me shall not walk in the
darkness, but shall have the light of life.
John 8:12

I am the resurrection and the life;
he who believes in me shall live even if he dies
John 11:25

"I am the way, and the truth, and the life;
no one comes to the Father, but through me.
John 14:6

Jesus is the only way to God and the fulfillment of our potential and those amazing promises.

How do we bring Jesus into our lives?

HOW TO FIND JESUS

Our salvation is through faith alone, through our commitment to Jesus Christ, 'the way, the truth and the life'.

God wants a personal relationship with all of us. We all have a choice to believe in God and also to seek His presence in a personal relationship. He will be there if we ask Him and our blessings will know no end.

By faith in Jesus Christ we receive all of God's promises. Jesus perfectly revealed the character of God, the glory of God, the power of God and the reality of God. Jesus is alive and the amazing promises we've been given are manifested in Him and His love.

It comes purely through our belief in Jesus Christ and commitment to His commands and authority in our lives.

You can turn to Jesus at any time in your life. Tell Him you are sorry for all the things you have done which you know you shouldn't have done. It doesn't matter what it is, if you really mean it, in that moment you are forgiven.

A simple prayer like this will suffice:-

> *Holy Father God, I know that I have done many things that are wrong in my life. I want you to know that I am truly sorry. Please forgive me and show me how to live in the light of your love. I invite your son Jesus Christ to become the Lord of my Life, to rule and reign in my heart from this day forward. Please send your Holy Spirit into my life to help me to live according to your will and your plans for me. In Jesus' name I pray. Amen*

Be prepared for a sensation of the Holy Spirit as you say this, a sense of God's presence. You may feel a sense of overwhelming emotion or a simple feeling of peace.

It doesn't matter who we are or what our lives have been, or what we have done, we only have to believe and commit our lives to Jesus to receive the grace of God's mercy.

The amazing thing about God's promises is that it is never too late to start again. It is never too late to seek forgiveness and come to a life in Christ.

Forget the former things; do not dwell on the past. See, I am doing a new thing! Now it springs up; do you not perceive it? (Isaiah 43:18-19)

We all, every single one of us, have a chance to start again.

HOW TO DEVELOP A RELATIONSHIP WITH GOD

As Christians, we are called to obey God's most important commandments, as Jesus directed us:-

> *'Hear, O Israel: The Lord our God, the Lord is one. Love the Lord your God with all your heart and with all your soul and with all your mind and with all your strength. The second is this: Love your neighbor as yourself. There is no commandment greater than these.' (Mark 12:29-31)*

We develop our relationship with God through prayer, reading Scripture, attending church and our fellowship with other Christians. Once we become a Christian, we are connected to all Christians through the world in the Body of Christ.

> *Just as a body, though one, has many parts, but all its many parts form one body, so it is with Christ. For we were all baptized by one Spirit so as to form one body—whether Jews or Gentiles, slave or free—and we were all given the one Spirit to drink. Even so the body is not made up of one part but of many. (1 Cor 12:12-14).*

We can begin to understand God's will for our life as we spend more time with Him. Prayer is something that sustains us through difficult and dark times. Relationships that are not nurtured fail to flourish. It is exactly the same with God. Prayer helps us to develop an intimacy with God.

Prayer is our way of communicating with God, listening to Him and opening our lives to Him. It isn't exclusively reserved for members of the church hierarchy. We can be free and spontaneous, it doesn't matter what we say or how we say it, the important thing is that we do say it.

It is important to remember that becoming a Christian doesn't grant us immunity from hard times. People still die or get sick, relationships break up, jobs are lost.

Yet despite those trials our lives are richer than before. When facing challenges or experiencing problems we always have Jesus.

> *Come to me, all you who are weary and burdened, and I will give you rest. Take my yoke upon you and learn from me, for I am gentle and humble in heart, and you will find rest for your souls. For my yoke is easy and my burden is light.' (Matthew 11:28-30)*

Jesus is our protector, he is our hope for eternity and our refuge for today. We can ask Him to come into our lives and keep us safe. It doesn't guarantee us freedom from physical hardship but spiritually we cannot be harmed

If we knew it all now, if we had all the answers now, we would have no need for God. God doesn't want to just give us wisdom. God wants us to develop a personal relationship with Him. He wants us to trust in Him fully and to find that peace that only comes from total dependence on His love.

Chapter 2
OUR BEST FRIEND IS JESUS

How many friends do you have who can relate to every one of your struggles, read your mind, be always willing to listen to you, and be willing to die for you? Probably not many, but no matter who you are, you do have access to one friend like this: **Jesus.**

Jesus was sent to this earth. He walked around like you and I do. He ate food, swatted at bugs, and went to work just like the rest of us. He had struggles. He was tempted. He got tired. And ultimately, He died, just like the rest of us will. And He did all of this, in part, so that He could relate to every one of our struggles. He knows what we're going through. He's not some aloof god in the sky. He understands where you are because He's been there.

No human being could ever witness our every thought without becoming bored, irritated, or offended. Instead they would be contemplating their own steady stream of thoughts while reacting to the thoughts pouring from us. But Jesus has the supernatural ability to reside in our body, and He *does* witness our every thought. His love is intimate and extremely personal. Jesus is the only friend who can answer our heart's innermost cry.

And Jesus is always willing to listen to us. Even when we don't make sense, even when we are rambling, He is there with a steady ear. You can always call on Him, no matter what time it is or what mood you're in or how little time you have. You can talk to Him on the way to work. You can talk to Him when you can't sleep at night. You can talk to Him in the shower or in the elevator. You can talk to Him without even speaking aloud.

Jesus taught that the greatest love a man can have is to lay down his life for his friends. We might compare this to the bonds that are made when people risk their health to donate blood or organs to save the life of a loved one. Police officers who would take a bullet for a partner exhibit this level of love. Jesus willingly put His life in the hands of His enemies for you and me. It was worth it for Him, because He wanted to know us. And He wants to know you.

BEING HONEST WITH GOD

'Do not be anxious about anything, but in every situation, by prayer and petition, with

thanksgiving, present your requests to God'.
(Philippians 4:6)

So many of us mask our real feelings and go through the motions of pretending everything's OK. In reality, underneath it all we may be suffocating under the countless pressures of daily life with nowhere to turn. We are constantly assailed by innumerable anxieties, not knowing where or who to turn to.

Yet we do have someone who is always there for us at any time, someone who craves a relationship with us, who wants us to come to Him and pour out our innermost thoughts and feelings.

We have God.

He wants us to be truthful with Him about how we feel. We can laugh with Him, cry with Him, openly express our fears to Him. We can be angry with Him. We can, as the verse from Philippians shows us, present Him with all of our requests, no matter how trivial they may seem to us.

If you are angry over a broken marriage, a sudden bereavement or the loss of your job, take it to God. Be honest with him. You won't shock Him with what you have to say. As Psalm 139 tells us, God knows already. 'Before a word is on my tongue, you Lord, know it completely' (Psalm 139:4)

Talk to God, no matter what it is. Thank Him when you have been blessed, say sorry to Him when you have done wrong. Cry with Him and be angry with Him if you are overwhelmed by life. Let Him heal you, ask Him for help. Pray to Him.

God's love is unconditional; He won't turn you away.

You will find that the longer you walk with God, the more the innate anger and anxiety will dissipate to be replaced with His strength and peace.

Prayer Suggestion

Father God, you see my heart, you know all of my thoughts. I thank you for my blessings, I share my doubts and fears with you. Help me to grow closer to you Lord and be confident in knowing that however I feel you are listening. In Jesus' name I pray. Amen.

YOU MATTER TO GOD

Ephesians 1:4-6
"For he chose us in him before the creation of the world to be holy and blameless in his sight. In love he predestined us for adoption to sonship through Jesus Christ, in accordance with his pleasure and will— to the praise of his glorious

grace, which he has freely given us in the One
he loves.”

God said to the prophet Jeremiah, “Before I formed you in the womb I knew you.” It is the same with us. God designed you. He knows what's on your heart. He knows how many hairs are on your head. He knows you and He loves you and if you are a believer, that's because He chose you. (And if you're not a believer, but you feel God tugging at your heart, then that means He chose you too!)

He chose you to be holy and blameless. Now, we've all made mistakes. We've all done things that have hurt ourselves or others, so we're not blameless. That's why we need Jesus, who makes us holy in *God's* sight. Because, in LOVE, God predestined us to be adopted through Jesus Christ. The love of Jesus makes us God's adopted children. The love of Jesus makes us holy and blameless. And all of this is done according to God's will and with his pleasure!

Now, you can listen to people sing “Jesus Loves Me” until you grow deaf and still not believe it. That's because this love is a gift, and you need to receive it. You need to open yourself up to this love. Then, once you feel it, you will realize it's unlike any other thing you've ever felt. It is the love of your Creator, and once you've accepted it, nothing can come between you and it.

God created you. God is God. He wouldn't spend time crafting a completely unique soul if that person did not matter to Him. You do matter. He loves you. All you have to do is let the love in.

Prayer Suggestion

Lord I want to feel your love. I open up my heart and welcome your love. Please let me feel your presence. Please help me live my life the way that you, my Creator, designed me to live it. Amen.

WHO WE ARE IN CHRIST

> *2 Corinthians 5:17 : "Therefore if anyone is in Christ, the new creation has come: The old has gone, the new is here!"*

Living in Christ. Most of us know that Jesus Christ, the Son of God, is the Savior of the World but, we may not understand what the phrase 'who we are in Christ' actually means.

Jesus offers eternal life and a place in God's Kingdom to all who choose to accept Him as their Savior. He dispels the darkness in our lives 'I am the light of the world. Whoever follows me will never walk in darkness, but will have the light of life' (John 8:12).

Yet it's much more than that too.

In Christ we are reconciled to God. We have access to Him through the Holy Spirit who comes to dwell within us and imbue us with a blessed peace.

In Christ we are a new creation. We are set free from the old life that binds us to ingrained and sometimes debilitating habits.

In Christ we are complete. The sins that have separated us from God are dissolved in God's unconditional love.

In Christ we are righteous. We are set free from the condemnation and shackles of this world to walk a new path.

The wonderful promises of a life in Christ are open to all. If your spirit is tinged with the heavy darkness of despair, do not be afraid, your hope and salvation lies in Jesus Christ. All you have to do is turn to Him and give your life to the one who sacrificed His own, defeated death and came 'that they may have life, and have it to the full.' (John 10:10).

Prayer Suggestion

Heavenly Father, help me to open my life up to your son Jesus Christ and to understand who I am in Him. Let the light that shines in the darkness illuminate my world that I may be as one with You. Amen.

THE UNIQUENESS OF CHRIST

*Jesus answered, I am the way and the truth
and the life. No-one comes to the Father except
through me.' John 14:6*

Jesus Christ is our Savior. His life, death and
resurrection represent the hope for Christians all over
the world.

Jesus is unique.

He is the only way to God. God's promises are only
attained through our faith in His only son.

Born of a virgin, Jesus came to earth as a fragile baby
and lived among us as a man, a human being of flesh
and blood. He was fully God and yet also fully man.

Jesus healed the sick, brought hope to the
underprivileged in society, performed miracles and
taught us to love our neighbor as ourselves.

In Jesus we have a Savior who can truly empathize
with us. He has lived as one of us, he understands the
limitations of our mortal bodies. He was tempted yet
was without sin.

He understands our suffering. In the garden of
Gethsemane he twice begged God to take away the
imminent agony of His death upon the cross, yet
He was obedient to God's will. 'And being found

in appearance as a man, he humbled himself by becoming obedient to death— even death on a cross!' (Philippians 2:8)

On the cross, He cried out to God, abandoned to bear the full weight and agony of our sin.

He triumphed over death to rise again and give us the promise of eternal life.

There is nothing that we will experience in our lives that is beyond his comprehension. He loved us all so much that he died for us.

Savor that for a moment, you may need to ponder on it to take in the enormity of its true meaning.

Jesus Christ is unique. He is the light of the world, the bread of life, the way and the truth, the resurrection and the life.

Jesus Christ is the Savior of the world.

Prayer Suggestion

Lord Jesus, thank you for your sacrifice of love. Teach me to love like you, teach me to live like you, teach me to follow your light and walk along your path. Amen

OUR PARTNERSHIP WITH GOD

'For we are God's fellow-workers; you are God's field, God's building'

1 Corinthians 3:9.

Once we have stepped into partnership with God that relationship becomes the focus of our lives through Jesus Christ. We become, as the words of Paul in Corinthians so clearly state, God's co-workers.

We are in partnership with God. Doesn't that sound incredible?

This partnership extends to every area of our life, from our relationships through to our work and our leisure time. In particular it extends to our prayer life. Everything we do is for the glory of God and our whole attitude should reflect this.

If you choose to enter into this partnership don't be surprised if you are overwhelmed with a feeling of peace. God is by your side in everything you do and His Holy Spirit is within you.

You will find that living in God's light and according to His will imbues you with an unparalleled sense of safety. You can be confident in the knowledge that whatever challenges assail you in this uncertain and unpredictable world your partnership with God is your strength and your refuge.

Of course, our partnership with God doesn't mean we approach life with a blatant disregard for others. It means living as Jesus taught us to live, to love God with all of our heart and soul and to love our neighbor as ourselves.

It means forgiveness of others who may wrong you and equally as important, forgiveness of yourself.

'For it is God who works in you to will and to act according to His good purpose'. (Philippians 2:13). If you are living in accordance with God's will and His purpose for your life expect to be enriched in ways you could never have imagined.

Step out today into that partnership with our amazing Creator. You will never look back.

Prayer Suggestion

Heavenly Father, creator of our world, take my hand as I step out into partnership with you. Show me how to live according to your purpose for my life and let everything I do reflect the light of your son Jesus Christ. Amen.

ATTRIBUTES OF GOD

'….God is love. Whoever lives in love lives in
God, and God in him' 1 John 4:10

No matter what else God is, above everything He is
love. When we seek a relationship with God, we long
to get to know Him better and understand what exists
beyond that love. We can never truly understand God
but the Bible tells us of His attributes.

God is our Creator. He gave life to everything in our
universe. As humans we were created in His image
and through our faith are encouraged to be more like
Him.

God is wisdom. God cannot make mistakes; He
knows and wants what's best for all of us. God has a
plan for our lives, all we have to do is trust Him

God is Holy. His holiness is reflected in His pure
and loving nature. He is without sin and has no evil
thoughts.

God is infinite. He has no limits. He transcends time;
He simply is. In the stillness we may seek to draw
near to Him. 'Be still and know that I am God' (Psalm
46:10)

God is omniscient. The phrase 'I am with you always'
is repeated 22 times in the Bible. What a wonderful

guarantee we have that no matter what we may experience in our lives, God is by our side.

God is grace. It is not our actions that have earned us God's love. It is His grace. He loves and blesses us with gifts even though we may not deserve it at times. God's grace is available to us all through Jesus Christ.

God is faithful. He cannot lie. God will always keep His promises and never abandon us.

God is merciful. He forgives us our sins, He is slow to anger and abounding in love, He offers endless patience to all of us.

We have a loving and merciful God whose grace offers countless blessings and a unique peace in our lives. To know more of God we need only to allow our barriers to fall and turn to Him.

Prayer Suggestion

Father God, I long to know you but don't know where to begin. Help me to be worthy of your grace and to learn to accept the blessings of the Holy Spirit into my life. Be with me today as I start my journey into faith with you. Amen.

GOD'S CLEAR INSTRUCTIONS

'Now faith is being sure of what we hope for and certain of what we do not see' Hebrews 11:1

Coming to faith in Jesus Christ means surrendering our lives to God's will for us. That doesn't guarantee a stress free life.

We know that God has a plan for our lives but sometimes it can seem that his plan for us is completely different to the plan we had in mind for ourselves.

Perhaps it's a relationship that falls apart or a loved one who falls ill. Maybe it's our career plans that fall to pieces. Suddenly the path of our life is taking an opposite turn to what we had envisioned and at times it is tempting to take matters into our own hands.

Times like these call for patience and trust in God. We need faith to believe in him and patience to wait on his timing. We should remember that one thousand years to us may be like a day to our transcendent God.

On top of that, we need courage to obey him, to listen to his Holy Spirit within us.
If you feel God is calling you down a particular path listen to his voice. If the calling grows stronger, take a leap of faith into the unknown. Be courageous and obey him.

One thing we can be certain of. God will give us what we need when we need it, not what we want because our human nature tells us we want it. 'And we know that in all things God works for the good of those who love him, who have been called according to his purpose'. (Romans 8:28)

Living by faith may seem like a huge risk but if we step out in that faith we can be sure God will reveal his will to us and with it his blessings for our life.
Be sure of what you hope for and certain of what you do not see.

Prayer Suggestion
Heavenly Father, as I step out in faith, help me to discern your voice. Teach me to be certain of what I do not see and to have patience and trust in your timing. In Jesus' name I pray. Amen.

UNDERSTANDING THE BIBLE

> *"All Scripture is God-breathed and is useful for teaching, rebuking, correcting and training in righteousness." 2 Timothy 3:17*

The Bible is the Word of God. As Paul states in his letter to Timothy, it is 'God-breathed'.

As Christians, the Bible is our guide and blueprint for living. God gave us the Bible so we can study it and apply its meaning and principles to every aspect of our lives. The key to understanding the Bible is not education but obedience and acting on God's Word. When we do this the scriptures will *come alive* and then we will be able to hear and understand the voice of God in our lives. Look for God's instructions when you read the scriptures in the Bible.

The Bible itself is divided into two sections, the Old Testament and the New Testament.

The Old Testament was the Bible used by Jesus comprising 39 'books'. It is the history of God's chosen people and contains stories already familiar to us; stories such as Moses and the parting of the Red Sea, of David and Goliath and of Joseph. Sometimes we see a wrathful God yet the overall message is of God's timeless truths and ultimate love for his people.

The New Testament gives us the four gospels recounting the life of Jesus Christ together with a collection of additional 'books' and letters comprising 27 different sections in total. The New Testament brings the new covenant of God's love and forgiveness.

Christians use the Bible to pray, to teach and to learn. Through the Bible we can grow in our personal relationship with God and learn to live in the light of Jesus Christ. It assures us of our salvation and the promise of eternal life through faith in him. It is the only self-help manual we will ever need

As you begin to read the Bible, you'll venture into a whole new world, a world so different from the one we live in today, yet fundamentally so similar.

You'll learn of the life, death and resurrection of Jesus. You'll learn how to live by his truths.

And you'll marvel at its wisdom and wonder how you managed to live without this God-breathed work.

Prayer Suggestion

Father God, thank you for giving us your Word. Stay by my side as I learn from your wisdom and venture day by day into this new life in Jesus Christ. Amen.

THE PATH TO FORGIVENESS

> *"If we confess our sins, he is faithful and just and will forgive us our sins and purify us from all unrighteousness." 1 John 1:9*

When we become Christians, we are born anew into our life with Jesus Christ.

One of the first steps we must take is to seek forgiveness from God. However, insurmountable you feel your past mistakes nothing is too much for God. His love for you is unconditional.

God sees your heart. If you are sincere in your confession forgiveness is guaranteed. The slate is wiped clean. 'Come now, let us reason together, says the Lord. Though your sins are like scarlet, they shall be as white as snow; though they are red as crimson, they shall be like wool' (Isaiah 1:18).

It is as straightforward as that.

Once God has forgiven you, you must also forgive yourself; Jesus gave us salvation through his death upon the cross, there is no room for guilt. After all, if God has forgiven you, how can you not forgive yourself? That would imply an error of judgment on God's part and he is never wrong.

It's natural that sometimes the burden of our sins can sometimes lay heavy on us even when we have confessed them to God. If you are wracked with remorse or distress, take it to God in prayer. Spend as much time with him as you need. Seek his peace and reassurance. Allow the guilt to ebb away. Call upon Jesus to be your guide.

When we have God's forgiveness, we will sense a renewal in our lives, a fresh inpouring of the Holy Spirit and a blessed peace.

Prayer Suggestion

Lord, I come to you in repentance for the wrongs I have done. I have sinned against you and others and

I am truly sorry. Grant me forgiveness and help me to forgive those who have wronged me. I ask this in the name of Jesus Christ who died for us all for the forgiveness of sins. Amen.

Chapter 3
KEEP JESUS IN FIRST PLACE

W hat takes first place in your life? For many of us, our children come first. For others, the husband, wife, or significant other comes first. For some, it's the career or job. For some, it's health and fitness. For some, it's a passion, like music, or a sport, or writing. Some even put service to others in first place—they are constantly looking for ways to make the world a better place.

All of these things are good things. All of these things are important. But what if there was a way that we could be stronger and better for all of these things?

What would happen if we put Jesus in first place? We'd be better parents, better partners, better professionals, better musicians, better athletes, better writers, better citizens—the truth is that we'd be unstoppable.

Many of us have realized this. Many of us *have* given our lives to Jesus. Praise God! Many of us know that

Jesus is the most important thing in our lives. But then what? Then duties of life come calling. The kids are sick, the spouse gets laid off, the laundry piles up, the boss wants more of your time, the soup kitchen wants more of your time, and your local church wants you there seven days a week.

And you wonder just how exactly you're supposed to keep up. Well, you're not. You can't. When we start living for Jesus, and even more so when we've been doing it for a while, we sometimes forget that Jesus has to come first. We get so caught up in doing our best and serving others that we forget to spend time with Jesus. And then we become frustrated, overtired, anxious, and depressed.

We must keep Jesus in first place. Without Him, none of this other stuff matters. You *can* say no to others. You *can* say, "No. I'm not going to do that. I need to spend time with Jesus." Most of us know that we're supposed to spend time each morning in the Word, but this becomes so difficult in real life. But if we do it, real life becomes less difficult. Most of us know that we're supposed to rest once a week. But in real life, this seems impossible. If we don't do it, real life is impossible.

We need to keep Jesus first. It's the best thing we can do for Jesus. It's the best thing we can do for ourselves. It's the best we can do for our loved ones. It's the best thing we can do for our neighbors. It's the best thing we can do for the world. And it's the only way to lead a joyous, peaceful, fulfilled life.

GOD LOVES YOU AS HIS GREATEST CREATION

Genesis 1:26-28
"Then God said, 'Let us make man in our image, in our likeness, and let them rule over the fish of the sea and the birds of the air, over the livestock, over all the earth, and over all the creatures that move along the ground....'"

We sometimes tremble before God when we've done wrong, or are afraid to go to Him with our burdens. We may even turn from praising Him because we look at His many wonders and feel insignificant. But this goes against everything that He has told us about His love for us.

God created us in *His image.* Imagine that! He created us as a reflection of Himself – we are the greatest of all His creations, more powerful and beautiful and more wonderfully made than anything He created, including the sun and planets and all of the amazing varieties of plants, animals and creatures He has ever made.

God even told us to, *"Be fruitful and increase in number; fill the earth and subdue it."* He didn't choose any other creature for this momentous task. So the next time you feel small in God's eyes, remember that you are truly wonderfully made and cherished as God's image on earth.

Prayer Suggestion

Thank the Lord for His creation and your special role in it. Promise that You will return the blessing of being created in His image by bringing glory and honor to your Creator.

GOD KNOWS YOUR NAME

Luke 12:6-7
"What is the price of five sparrows—two copper coins? Yet God does not forget a single one of them. And the very hairs on your head are all numbered. So don't be afraid; you are more valuable to God than a whole flock of sparrows."

There's a song entitled, "His Eye is on the Sparrow." It reminds me of these verses. God values all life. He wouldn't let even a sparrow fall and be harmed.

Yet, He knows how many hairs are on our head. We are made in His image – every man, woman, boy and girl who lives now, have lived or will ever inhabit this earth mirror Him. He loves us even more than those birds.

Fame is something that people want in this world. They want to be noticed by someone, anyone. It can lead to the wrong road in life just for love and attention. God loves us so much that it pains Him when we turn to others for the love that only He can give.

That hole you feel can only be filled by Him. Once He enters your life, then real love can grow. We can learn how to love others and also how to be loved by others.

What do you have to lose? You trust other people who don't keep their promises. God will keep His. And, He knows you better than anyone else alive.

Prayer Suggestion

God knows your name, but do you know His? When you pray, say "Abba, Father." He will hear you and answer.

GOD KNOWS WHERE YOU ARE

Psalm 139:7
"I can never escape from your Spirit!
I can never get away from your presence!"

When you're a kid, no matter where you go, it seems like your parents can always tell where you are. It's that uncanny ability that amazes and frustrates you at the same time, especially when you don't want to be found. It's the same with God. He's our Heavenly

Father and He can always find us even if we don't want to be found.

In the verse above, it sounds like David is trying to escape from God. He realizes that it is useless and starts to yell in desperation. In actuality, he is happy that God can always find Him. You might not want to acknowledge it now, but when you are lost, all you want to be – is found.

God can see us when we sin and when we do good. Yes, He is disappointed when we don't follow Him, but in His love, He still protects us. And, most importantly, He is always, always ready to accept us back into His fold.

When we do find God again, we are often scared to tell Him what we've been doing. Here's a news flash: He already knows. He sees what we do in the light and the dark. It is not God's nature to want to crush us in our sin or ridicule us for what we've done.

Yes, He wants us to confess our sins to Him but because we love and trust Him, not because He's ignorant of what we've been up to. And, He will forgive and gather us up into His loving arms to be comforted – forever. How's that for a welcome home greeting!

Prayer Suggestion

God is always watching you – with love in His heart.

GOD WILL GIVE YOU A NEW BEGINNING

2 Corinthians 5:17
"This means that anyone who belongs to Christ has become a new person. The old life is gone; a new life has begun!"

Have you ever wished that you could have a "do over"? Kids often say this when they make a mistake playing a game. They just start again as if the unfortunate incident never happened.

As you get older, this concept takes on new meaning. As adults, we lack the childlike freedom that a "do over" can bring. We just don't believe that such things are possible anymore.

God is in the "do over" business. When you accept Jesus Christ into your life, you get a second chance to make a first impression. Some of us may be thinking like Nicodemus when he asked Jesus if a man could reenter the womb and be born again. Our new beginning comes in the form of a spiritual birth that changes us from the inside out.

Our past wrongs are forgiven. Unlike people who can hold a grudge for years, God simply forgets our wrongs and lovingly gives us a new path to follow. It seems too incredible to believe but God is not complicated.

This change isn't about feelings but about focus. As long as we strive and desire to take our lead from God, He is faithful to give us a clean heart and a new lease on life. Others may notice it in us before we do. God doesn't change our appearance, but people do "see" us differently.

Are you tired of living a life of defeat and regret? Go to God and ask for a new life.

Prayer Suggestion

Create in me a clean heart, Lord. I know that if You change me I will be changed forever.

PEACE WITH GOD

> **Philippians 4:5-7**
> *"The Lord is near. Do not be anxious about anything, but in every situation, by prayer and petition, with thanksgiving, present your requests to God. And the peace of God, which transcends all understanding, will guard your hearts and your minds in Christ Jesus."*

Isaiah 9:6 calls Jesus the Prince of Peace. There is a reason for this. Once we know Christ, we don't need to suffer from a lack of inner peace anymore.

Of course, the world will rage on around us, and many of us will find ourselves in less than peaceful circumstances, but we can still have peace on the inside, because God has promised us that He will protect us, care for us, and even glorify us.

This doesn't necessarily mean that it will be easy. Some of us are simply prone to be anxious. But this doesn't mean we can't seek this transcendent peace.

The first step is believing that the Lord is near. If you train your mind to remind you of this whenever you feel anxious, anxiety loses a lot of its power. You're stuck in traffic. You're late. You're going to get hollered at when you get to work. But the Lord is near. Doesn't that knowledge take the power out of your situation?

Once we recognize that the Lord is near, then we need to start working on bringing everything to God in prayer. Many of us have (erroneously) been taught that God doesn't want to hear about our little problems. How can we pray about our boss hollering at us when there are hungry children all over the world? But this view is not Scriptural. God *does* want us to bring *all* of our problems to him, no matter what size they are.

It is through this process, by laying our needs at God's feet, that we start to experience peace with God. We are not designed to carry these worries around. We are designed to give them to our Designer.
You can have peace with God. You can be free of unrest. You are invited to rest safely in God's arms.

Prayer Suggestion

Thank you, Heavenly Father, for listening to my prayers and petitions. Please give me your peace. I want to rest in your arms. Amen.

THE SOURCE OF OUR STRENGTH

Philippians 4:13
"I can do all things through Him who strengthens me."

The Greek word that is translated "strengthen" in this verse literally means "to put power in." God puts power in us. This is the source of our strength.

But we have to let Him do it. When everything is going along wonderfully, we tend to think we can do it all on our own, and we do not draw on this source of strength. Then, when things aren't so great, we feel weak, and we wonder why? We have to *let Him strengthen us*. God is a gentleman—he's not going to pump us full of power against our will.

There's a reason that Paul wrote, in 2 Corinthians 12:10, "for when I am weak, then I am strong." In order to experience the full power of God's strength, we need to recognize our need for it, ask for it, believe for it, and accept it when it comes.

Have doubts? No problem—ask God to deliver you from your doubts. He will.

There are ways we can open ourselves up to this source of strength. Spending time in the Word will always make us stronger. You don't have to spend all day reading the Bible, but set aside a few minutes where the Bible is all that you will do. Read and reflect and ask God to show you what He wants you to know in that moment.

Another way to spend time with God is through music. Music that is created for the glory of Christ can be a tremendous source of strength for Christ's followers.

And of course, don't underestimate the power source that prayer is. Spend some time just talking with God. Tell Him how you're feeling, what you're struggling with. Having trouble articulating your thoughts and feelings? Don't worry—the Bible tells us that when we're not sure what to say, the Holy Spirit is there to help. Romans 8:26 tells us that the Holy Spirit "helps our weakness; for we do not know how to pray as we should, but the Spirit Himself intercedes for us with groanings to deep for words." You're carrying around your own translator!

Prayer Suggestion

Heavenly Father, thank you for being the source of my strength. Please make me strong. Help me to trust in you and to draw on your strength, every day. Amen.

GOD IS A GUIDING LIGHT

> **Exodus 13:21**
> "*The* LORD *went ahead of them. He guided them during the day with a pillar of cloud, and he provided light at night with a pillar of fire. This allowed them to travel by day or by night.*"

Have you ever noticed how dark it gets outside at night? If you've ever walked down a dirt road near dusk, when the sun goes down it's like a blanket being pulled over your head. If you weren't actually walking, you wouldn't know up from down.

Walking in darkness is a scary experience that we wouldn't want to experience more than once. Yet, many of us live in darkness every day of our lives. It's time to turn on the light inside of you and see what's going on.

King David remarked that the Word of God was a "lamp" and a "light" for him. It illuminated his way in an otherwise dark world. God's Word is still a guiding light to you today. His principles are eternal.

The verse for today refers to the exodus of the Israelites from Egypt. In the desert there are no lights. In order for the people to keep traveling they needed to see where they were going. God provided that light so they would not end up going in circles. Studying the Word of God today keeps you from going around in circles in your life.

One way that God leads is through the pages of the Bible. How do you handle temptation? Call on God for help and He promises to make a "way of escape." What about planning for the future? Seek God first and He will guide you into making the right decisions for your life.

All of these answers come out of the Bible. It is a roadmap lighting the way towards abundance in this life and the next. And, abundance is overflowing blessing in every area of your life.

Prayer Suggestion

Ask God to shine a light on areas of your life that need His attention.

THE POWER OF KINDNESS – THE GOD PRINCIPLE

Luke 6:37–38

"Do not judge others, and you will not be judged. Do not condemn others, or it will all come back against you. Forgive others, and you will be forgiven. Give and you will receive. Your gift will return to you in full—pressed down, shaken together to make room for more, running over, and poured into your lap. The amount you give will determine the amount you get back."

The world is desperately in need of a new way of thinking. Often the Word of God is perverted with such sayings as "do unto others before they can do unto you." The mentality of some is to do whatever it takes to reach the top. You can ask the ones who have been jailed for criminal schemes how it works for them now.

Why is kindness and grace withheld from others when God has been so generous? Maybe you have been hurt by someone at some point. The human response would be to mistrust others. Jesus was treated badly, but he still prayed for his offenders.

The God Principle is contrary to anything that the world is teaching. With the God Principle, gaining favor in your life is dependent on what you do for others. See, most people give that same look when they hear it. Jesus, the Son of God, took off his tunic and washed the feet of his disciples. A foot washing was thought to be menial work. Jesus saw it as serving others and therefore serving God.

God wants us to share what He has done for us with others. Every time we extend a helping hand to someone, whether they deserve it or not in our minds, God is honored and a life is changed. Because you are being obedient, God will bless your life in untold ways. Kindness has its privileges.

Prayer Suggestion

Ask God to put people in your path today who need to see Jesus.

HAVE YOU FLED THE LORD?

> *Jonah 1:1-17*
> *"…The word of the Lord came to Jonah son of Amittai, "Go to the great city of Ninevah and preach against it, because its wickedness has come up before me.'*
> *But Jonah ran away from the Lord….and sailed for Tashish to flee the Lord."*

Most of us can sympathize with Jonah in the passage above. It is instinct to run away when we have something unpleasant to face, and Jonah knew that no one would want to hear a prophesy of doom in Ninevah. Did he turn down God's request? No! He simply ran away from his duty to God, yet God pursued him.

There is nowhere you can go to outrun God, nothing you can do to turn God away from His purpose for you. This is where many of us fail as Christians. We try to bend God to our will instead of submitting our wills to God. We are willing to serve God – as long as it isn't too inconvenient, dangerous or embarrassing!

Yet the harder you work to get away from God's plan for you, the more earnestly God will seek you out. He has laid the plans for your life at the beginning of time and you cannot hide from your purpose. Don't force God's hand – you could end up, like Jonah, in a whale of a mess! If, instead, you graciously accept God's design for your life, you will soon discover that the path is laid straight for you and you will achieve all God asked of you and more.

Prayer Suggestion

Ask God to reveal His plan for you, then stand strong and commit to it. Make a vow to stop trying to run away from God in times of trouble.

WHY SHOULD YOU GO TO CHURCH?

Hebrews 10:24-25
"And let us consider how we may spur one another on toward love and good deeds. Let us not give up meeting together, as some are in the habit of doing, but let us encourage one another – and all the more as you see the Day approaching."

Some Christians attend church faithfully, while others argue that since we can commune privately with God, church is an outdated notion that doesn't mean anything. But in his letter to the Hebrews, the writer above explains just how important regularly getting together with other Christians is.

Starting each week with church grounds you by giving you a firm basis in scripture for the rest of your week. It's a reminder of what is truly important in God's eyes. Starting your week with praise and worship is uplifting. Worship is also a form of sacrifice – you are giving yourself over to God each Sunday, acknowledging His central role in your life.

Congregating with other Christians also allows us to help each other and uphold each other in times of crisis. If you attend church regularly, you will be surrounded by a strong family of believers in times of trouble. Without a church family, you may stumble and fall or turn to non-Christians who will lead you away from God.

Prayer Suggestion

Thank the Lord for the opportunity to meet and become friends with others in a Christian setting each week. Renew your resolve to sacrifice a few hours each week to the Lord by attending church regularly.

THE GOD CHALLENGE – ARE YOU BEING FRUITFUL?

Philippians 2:1-4
"Now if you have known anything of Christ's encouragement and of his reassuring love; if you have known something of the fellowship of his Spirit, and of compassion and deep sympathy, do make my joy complete--live together in harmony, live together in love, as though you had only one mind and spirit between you. Never act from motives of rivalry or personal vanity, but in humility think more of each other than you do of yourselves. None of you should think only of his own affairs, but consider other people's interests also."

God doesn't want us to simply love Him in our hearts. He also wants us to show the world, through every act and deed as well as our words, our loving relationship with Him. Many times people who aren't Christians look at those who are and think, "They talk about dedication to God, but they are a lot of talk and not much action."

Look at your life today and ask yourself, "Was I a blessing to others today? Did I demonstrate my love of the Lord to others through how I treated them? Was I truly fruitful, or was I simply busy?"

There is a big difference between keeping ourselves busy with activities that are centered on our own desires and truly being fruitful Christians who are cultivating His love on earth. God challenges us every day to look *beyond* simply getting through each day and work toward making each day an opportunity to help others, bless others and pray for others. Have you taken up God's challenge today?

Prayer Suggestion

Pray for others before yourself. Ask the Lord to reveal to you ways that you can be fruitful in your everyday life, dedicating yourself to "thinking more of others than yourself."

GOD LOVES OUR QUESTIONS

Psalm 13:1-6
"How long, O Lord? Will you forget me forever?
How long will you hide your face from me?
How long must I wrestle with my thoughts
And every day have sorrow in my heart?
How long will my enemy triumph over me?

Look on me and answer, O Lord my God.
Give light to my eyes, or I will sleep in death;
My enemy will say, 'I have overcome him,'
And my foes will rejoice when I fall.

But I trust in your unfailing love;
My heart rejoices in your salvation.
I will sing to the Lord,
For He has been good to me."

Sometimes we are afraid to ask God questions, fearing that we are being disrespectful and betraying Him. But God welcomes our questions! Even King David, one of God's greatest kings and a righteous man, asks God uncomfortable questions in the psalm above. But read it carefully and you will see that after he questions God, he admits that, even in the face of the many fears and questions he has for God, he still trusts in Him and rejoices in God's grace.

So is it okay to ask questions? Yes! God delights in our questions because it shows that we are seeking Him, seeking understanding, and seeking answers for our lives. The key that we need to remember is that we must learn to accept God's answers. They may not be the answers we hope for, and they may not be comfortable answers, but we will receive answers in God's time and according to God's plan.

So do not turn from God because you don't feel worthy to ask questions. It's what God wants. He wants us to ask Him the tough questions so that He can give us the answers we seek. And while we are waiting for those answers, we should continually praise Him and thank Him for giving us questioning hearts so that we can draw closer to Him.

Prayer Suggestion

Lay your questions before God, asking Him the questions that you have been afraid to put before Him. Give thanks for His infinite wisdom in allowing us to ask questions in order to know Him more intimately.

GET TO KNOW GOD BETTER

Philippians 4:8

"Finally, brothers, whatever is true, whatever is noble, whatever is right, whatever is pure, whatever is lovely, whatever is admirable—if anything is excellent or praiseworthy—think about such things."

The more we get to know God, the more we want to know Him. So how do we start? He's made it somewhat simple for us. He's given us options.

Scripture. The key to God's heart is written in His Holy Word, and by reading it and meditating on it, we will get to know God better.

Prayer. When you want to get to know another person, don't we usually start with conversation? The same goes for God. Talk to God. He's always listening.

Meditation. You don't have to sit with your legs crossed underneath you and rock back and forth. You can meditate on good things on your commute to work, or before you fall asleep at night. The Bible just tells us to think about good things, things that are noble, right, pure, lovely, and admirable. That is a pleasant command to follow! Think about good things? It's that easy?

Nature. We can get to know God better by taking a walk through the woods, or the park, or by putting some freshly cut flowers on our dining room table. God created the world in all its beauty for us to enjoy, and for us to know Him through. By gazing up at the stars, we get a glimpse of Who God can be.

Solitude. Solitude is more difficult for some of us than for others. Some of us have noisy, busy jobs. Some of us have toddlers running around the house. But all of us would be better off if we took a few minutes out of our day to be alone with God. To be silent, to stare at the stars, or at the grass, or at the snow, and to pray, and to think about good things.

Prayer Suggestion

"God, help me get to know You better. Help me find You in my life, in Your Word, in Your world, and in my heart."

GOD SPEAK TO ME

> ***Romans 10:17***
> *"Consequently, faith comes from hearing the message, and the message is heard through the word of Christ."*

I've heard people say that God has become silent. I wonder ... if we're not hearing God, is it because we're not listening? There is a lot of noise in this world. There is a lot to keep us distracted, to keep us busy, to keep us from listening.

So how do we listen? Through the Bible. God's Word is a living Word that will speak to us if we just open it and read. We need to pray that God will reveal Himself and His will to us through his Holy Scripture.

How else can we listen? We can literally listen by going to where the Word of God is preached. This can be a church service, a Bible study, a gathering of friends, or a retreat.

God is not silent, even when we think He is. There is always the Word to return to. By prayerfully considering the Scripture, by reading and listening to the Word, God's will can and will be revealed to us.

Sometimes there is something in our lives standing between God and ourselves. If that something is not glorifying God, then we should probably let go of it. This can be painful and difficult, but imagine the relief when, once it's gone, God's voice rings out loud and clear!

I've heard many people testify that once they truly humbled themselves and came before God, sincerely asking to hear His voice, God spoke. Suddenly they flopped their Bible open to what seemed like a random page, and there was the verse they needed at that moment. Then the next day, that just happened to be the verse the pastor preached on. Sometimes God speaks through coincidences.

Prayer Suggestion

God is speaking. We just need to listen. And if you can't hear Him right now, then pray. Pray with conviction. Pray, "Lord, let me hear your beautiful voice. Speak to me God. Teach me how to listen to You." And He will.

Chapter 4
TRUST IN GOD

When we are really struggling with life, sometimes the last words we want to hear are "Just trust in God, everything will be alright." This just sounds like cheap, empty, fluffy advice meant to stop us from whining. Has anyone ever said something like this to you? Have you ever wanted to say, "Trust in God? Seriously? Where was God when I got into this mess?" If so, you are not alone.

But we need to remember that God *was* right there when we got into this mess. And there *is* a purpose to this mess! Though we couldn't possibly untangle the yarn right now, God is actually knitting a beautiful sweater out of this knot!

The Bible tells us that God causes all things to work together for good to those who love Him. So even when you can't find a job, when your child is sick, when you're grieving the loss of a loved one, when you're facing bankruptcy, when you're battling addiction—

even *then*, in that mess, in that tightly tangled knot, God *is* working for your good. Of course you don't know what good is coming. Of course you don't understand. If you did, you wouldn't need to trust God, and God wants us to learn to trust Him.

Think of poor Job from the Old Testament. He lost all of his possessions, all of his wealth, all of his loved ones, and he was sick and in pain. (And then his friends showed up to torture him with awful advice.) How many of us would have continued to trust God in those circumstances? But Job did, even though he didn't understand. And because he trusted God, he was blessed beyond measure for the rest of his life.

And because he trusted God, millions of people have been inspired, comforted, and taught by Job's story. Even if Job had been told that this would be the reason for his suffering, it wouldn't have made any sense—Job couldn't possibly imagine a world where millions of people would be able to read his story. And yet we can. And God knew this.

God knows things we don't know. We know this. Yet sometimes, in the heat of the moment, we forget. We must trust that God knows what He is doing. God sees the big picture. God will take care of us. And someday, we're going to look back on all of this and have a much better understanding. And we'll be glad that we trusted.

ASK GOD FOR HELP

> **Psalm 121:1-2**
> *"I look up to the mountains—does my help come from there?*
> *My help comes from the LORD, who made heaven and earth!"*

Everyone needs help. We were put on this earth to help one another. Asking for help is another story entirely.

Depending on which generation you grew up in, there are all sorts of reasons to ask for or not to ask for help. Here's one that is particularly wrong that many people believe: "Only weak people ask for help. If you are strong, you don't need it." That sounds like advice from way back. It needs to stay there.

In the New Testament, Jesus told the people that he came to seek and to save that which was lost. If you are lost, how are you going to find your way without help? On a trip, you may not ask for directions and eventually find your way, taking the roundabout route. There's no harm or foul here except lost time. In your life, not seeking God's help can lead to all sorts of situations that may prove disastrous and have lasting effects.

The best thing about seeking God's help is that you don't have to fill out a requisition form or make an appointment to get a little bit of His time. There are no rules except that you believe He exists and longs to do what is best for you. Talk to God in the shower, as you look for a parking spot at the grocery store, in the car, while cleaning, and anywhere else you happen to be.

It is not weakness to ask an Almighty God for help. In fact, it is pretty smart. When you want to know something, you go to the One who knows it all. Now your decisions will be built on a sure foundation. He will change your life into something that you never thought it could be.

Prayer Suggestion

Prayer is a conversation with God. Strike one up with Him throughout the day to stay connected to His Power.

GOD UNDERSTANDS IT ALL

John 3:16-17
"For God loved the world so much that he gave his one and only Son, so that everyone who believes in him will not perish but have eternal life. God sent his Son into the world not to judge the world, but to save the world through him."

It may seem at times that you are all alone in your agony. Friends and family just don't seem to "get it." Have you considered God?

He knows all about this world we live in and the pressures and problems we face. Because the world is not perfect, living in it is a challenge. That is why God sent Jesus to show us how to live at peace with and have victory in the here and now. Being an all-knowing God, He knew the outcome of sending his Son to live among a fallen generation. And, He sent him anyway.

Jesus lived as we live: He grew from a baby, living with parents who were not the wealthiest people around. He had to live with brothers and sisters and you know how that can be. He dealt with prejudice, disease, despair, hunger, death and heartache. It sounds like many of the issues that we deal with in our lives.

Jesus knew firsthand what type of toll these situations and others could have on the mind and the body. Through his connection with God, he faced them through prayer and time alone with Him. His life serves as an example of how we are to live in the world today. Yes, Jesus lived on earth over 2,000 years ago but human nature has not changed in all that time. Despair is still despair.

God knows intimately what you go through on a daily basis. He is there at every turn just waiting for you to seek His love and guidance. He gave His Son for the chance to hear and help you. He loves you that much.

Prayer Suggestion

Pray that God will share His wisdom with you and bring peace in difficult times.

CHRISTIAN DETOURS

> **Matthew 26:41**
> *"Keep watch and pray, so that you will not give in to temptation. For the spirit is willing, but the body is weak!"*

Have you heard the adage, "You can lead a horse to water, but you can't make him drink"? Sometimes it rightly describes us in our lives. Our parents (or guardians) teach us from childhood to discern right from wrong. They can't expose us to every situation in life, but they do give us that foundation.

It is human nature to be led by your emotions. The book of Romans tells us that "everyone has sinned." It is that sin that God wiped out with Jesus' sacrifice. But, while we are living on this earth, there is still the fleshly nature to contend with.

There is a common misconception that when you accept God into your life, you become perfect right then and there. For non-believers, they think people become Christian "robots," brainwashed to do God's will. Neither of these things is true.

How many of us, if given the choice, would choose to take the easy way out in every situation? God's word says that we are saved when we confess His existence and repent of our sins. But that is only the beginning. Without daily contact with God, we will still look for those "detours" in life instead of following His path.

As we spend time with God, He teaches us His "right and wrong" through His Word. A new foundation is established. Just like an earthly parent teaches, there will be consequences for disobedience. It is the firm hand of love and not disgust that guides us towards obedience and eternal life.

Prayer Suggestion

God's discipline is far better than the world's. Ask forgiveness for disobedience and learn from God's loving reproof.

EMBRACE GOD'S SILENCE

Palm 46:10
"Be still, and know that I am God! I will be honored by every nation. I will be honored throughout the world."

Have you ever had the "silent treatment" from someone? It mostly happens when you are kids in school. The first thing you do is wonder what you did wrong to deserve such a cold shoulder from someone who was talking to you the day before.

Sometimes it can feel like we are getting the "cold shoulder" from God. We wait to hear from Him and are met with our own thoughts. Unlike the immature attitude adopted when we were kids, God's silence is not a punishment or a thoughtless act.

The current generation seems to hate silence. Each and every day is filled with noises of some kind. We'd rather talk to ourselves than be surrounded by the loudness of quiet.

Why does God allow such moments, especially when He can see that we are in distress? It is a tool that teaches us to listen to the Spirit within us. We definitely know how to talk, but do we know how to hear?

When your world seems to be spinning out of control, you panic and the last thing you want to encounter is the closed doors of heaven. But, the adage goes, "When a door closes, God always opens a window." In this case, the window of your mind needs to be open.

It is in those silent, peaceful moments that the Spirit reminds us how good God has been in our life. What has He delivered you from before? Didn't He meet your needs at every turn? Now your soul is calmed knowing that there is not a situation in your life that God can't handle.

God might be silent(working everything out for our good) but He is *never* absent in our lives.

Prayer Suggestion

Make time to listen to the Spirit each day and rediscover God's goodness in the silence.

GOD DOES NOT HAVE A PLAN B

> *Jeremiah 29:11*
> *"For I know the plans I have for you," says the* LORD. *"They are plans for good and not for disaster, to give you a future and a hope."*

In our world there is something called a "contingency plan." In case our first efforts don't work out, we have another plan to fall back on. You are hedging your bets so to speak.

God's doesn't have a contingency plan nor does He need one. That alone makes some people suspicious of Him. *What if this God thing doesn't work out? What if I can't keep from sinning? What then?*

In the book of Jeremiah, God uses the prophet to

reassure the people. They were living in troubled times. Jerusalem had been destroyed, but God was not going to leave them destitute. If they chose to follow Him again, He would restore them.

God is giving that same message to you today. Turn from your sinful living and embrace His Word. Even in our waywardness God has a plan for our lives, but it can't be realized until we surrender our plans for His.

When you were growing up, your parents made the decisions for you. You didn't think about "Plan B" because you trusted them. Remember that child-like trust when you think of your Heavenly Father. He will carry you through the storms of life. When you fall, He will pick you up.

Instead of second guessing, go to God. Leave the heavy work to Him and rest in the knowledge that He has it all under control.

Prayer Suggestion

It is not easy to trust. But as you live for God day by day, He will show you that He is all that you need.

GOD DOES NOT SHOW US EVERYTHING

1 Corinthians 13:12

"Now we see things imperfectly as in a cloudy mirror, but then we will see everything with perfect clarity. All that I know now is partial and incomplete, but then I will know everything completely, just as God now knows me completely."

The thirteenth chapter of First Corinthians is about love. It is not the hand-holding kind of love but the love that God has for us that was demonstrated by Christ. It is the kind of love that we are told to have one for another.

The goal of science is to discover the mysteries of our world. We have come a long way from the age of dinosaurs. Who would ever have thought that we would be able to travel beyond this planet and move amongst the stars. But, it didn't happen overnight. It was a process.

The same is true with God. We can't always see the end of the road but we know it is there. One day at a time, God lays the foundation in our lives. Each day gives us hope for the future and, eventually we find out what God wanted us to see.

There is a danger in knowing the end result at the beginning. You never learn anything. God wants to empower us and that comes through faithful obedience that everything will be revealed in due course.

Who knows? That student you tutored patiently in math may one day become a great teacher, helping other students.

Prayer Suggestion

Lord, help me not be anxious about what you ask me to do today. Let me trust and leave the outcome to You.

GOD HAS A PRUNING PROCESS

> *Proverbs 25:4*
> *"Remove the dross from the silver, and out comes material for the silversmith."*

When gardeners prune bushes, they cut off dead or unsightly branches. They do this for two reasons: to make the bush more beautiful, and to improve growth.

God does the same thing with us. He helps us to get rid of our dead branches, those things that have become part of us through life's trials. You know, the baggage we all carry around. Sometimes, we are reluctant to let go of it, but it is this baggage, these dead or unsightly limbs, that keeps us from flourishing in God's grace. If we allow God to prune away these dead branches, we will be more ready and able to grow in our faith, and to grow as beautiful individuals designed in God's image, for God's purpose. Do we really want dead branches getting in the way of such lofty goals?

This verse from Proverbs compares us to silver. A silversmith has to heat up his metal, so that the dross will rise to the top, and he can scrape it off. Sometimes God will apply a little pressure, a little heat, to our lives, so that our dross will become more visible, and He can help us scrape it off. Then we are ready to be molded by the silversmith, by God. Then we are ready to be beautiful, pure, gleaming silver, reflecting the light of God's grace.

Change is difficult, but do any of us really want dead branches in our lives? Wouldn't any of us rather be heated up a little if it makes us shine more brightly?

Prayer Suggestion

"Dear Lord, please prune me for Your purpose. I want to shine in Your grace."

MOVING FORWARD BY FAITH

Romans 12:2

"Do not conform any longer to the pattern of this world, but be transformed by the renewing of your mind. Then you will be able to test and approve what God's will is—his good, pleasing and perfect will."

Be transformed. By the renewing of your mind. Sounds awesome, doesn't it? People pay big bucks to therapists for transformation and renewing of the mind. But real transformation, real renewal, comes from God.

Not conforming to the pattern of this world does not mean that believers cannot live in the world, cannot enjoy the world. God created the world for us to enjoy. It's the destructive patterns of the world that God frees us from. The cycles of fear and hatred. The greed and envy. Believers are transformed away from these destructive forces, and towards a new life of peace, love, and joy. In this new life, we get to experience God's will for us, his good and perfect will. It is this new form of ourselves that gets to move forward on faith.

Once we are renewed, once we are transformed, we are invited to move forward, stepping out of ourselves and our human limitations and into God's will. Sounds exciting, doesn't it?

Have you ever seen a mustard seed? Ever held one in the palm of your hand? Tiny, isn't it? The Bible tells us that if we have faith as small as a mustard seed, we can say to a mountain, "Get out of my way," and it will move. The Bible tells us that with faith as tiny as a mustard seed, nothing will be impossible for us. Because we have been transformed. Because we are no longer conformed to the patterns of this world. Because the truth has set us free. Free to move forward toward the awesome individuals God planned us to be, for the good purposes of His will.

Prayer Suggestion

"Dear Lord, Please give me the courage to be transformed, to walk away from the patterns of this world and to walk towards Your love and Your will. Help me to move forward on faith."

GOD ALWAYS KEEPS HIS PROMISES

Acts 2:39
"For the promise is unto you, and to your children, and to all that are afar off, even as many as the LORD our God shall call."

In the book of Acts, Peter delivers a promise to the people directly from God. Most people are familiar with verse 38, but not necessarily the one that comes after. He was talking about salvation and how it is available to everyone.

Many things in our lives are temporary; we just don't always know it. Jobs that seem permanent go away when the economy gets bad. Love relationships go sour. Unfortunately, it is the nature of this world.

God is not of this world. He created this world. His son, Jesus, came to let us know how much we are loved by the Father. Part of that love comes in the form of promises.

But, how many of us actually believe them? Living this life can make you cynical and untrusting of those who make promises – even God. But, the Father is patient with us. Because He is God, He cannot lie to us like other humans can and do.

In the promise above, when you call on God through repentance and participate in the act of baptism, the Holy Spirit will inhabit your soul and guide your life. You will be in the palm of His hand where no one can steal your joy or your salvation unless you let them.

Standing on the promises that cannot fail,
When the howling storms of doubt and fear assail,
By the living Word of God I shall prevail,
Standing on the promises of God.
                              –R. Kelso Carter, 1886

Prayer Suggestion

If God promises it to you, it will come to pass.

GOD IS OUR SUSTAINER

> **Philippians 4:6**
> *"Don't worry about anything; instead, pray for everything. Tell God what you need, and thank him for all he has done."*

What is the reason that you get out of bed in the morning? Of course you have to go to work so that you can make money but what drives you to even do that?

Think about lifting a heavy load. It might be awkward in shape and throw you off balance. But, when someone else helps you carry that load, it doesn't seem so heavy and you can regain your center. God is a lot like that person who comes along to help shoulder the load. The difference being that instead of carrying the load itself, He carries you.

How does He carry us, you might ask? It is through the power of the Holy Spirit. When Jesus was preparing for his crucifixion, he told his disciples that when he went away God would send them a Comforter. That is the spirit of God that inhabits every believer when they ask Him into their lives.

The Comforter is God's promise to you of His presence always and through every problem that you face. People have described the spirit as a "still small voice" or a kind of "knowing." However, God manifests Himself in your life it is first and foremost an act of faith. Without believing in His care and love, He could do nothing to enhance your life.

In Hebrew, Jehovah Jireh means "Lord God, Our Provider." Abraham coined this phrase when he was given a ram in the bush to sacrifice instead of his son, Isaac. In your life, there has been more than one "ram in the bush" that God has provided – you just didn't know it. When you give your life to Him, the reality of all that God does in your life is revealed. You'll wonder how you ever lived without Him.

Prayer Suggestion

Instead of asking God to remove your mountains, ask Him to carry you over them.

FILLING THE VOID WITH GOD

Matthew 6:33
"Seek the Kingdom of God above all else, and live righteously, and he will give you everything you need."

Have you ever received a package? When it is delivered, the package is heavy because it is filled with something. When you remove what's inside, the box is empty. It usually ends up thrown out with the trash.

There are people who feel that their lives are like that box. You might even feel that way. At one time, life seemed full, but then what gave them purpose was taken away leaving only emptiness. Suicide is like an empty life thrown on the trash heap.

Jesus told his disciples that they would encounter all manner of problems and desperate situations in their walk with him through the world, but to hold on to hope. At the time, He knew something that they didn't. His death would serve to break the hold that Satan and this life have on us all.

Living in this world is not for the faint of heart. Nothing, even the things that we believe to be, is ever certain. In the Sermon on the Mount, Jesus told the listeners to store up treasures for themselves in Heaven. Now, that's a long way to go for a storage space.

But, you don't have to travel anywhere. The storage space is located inside of you. Think about it: Every day, we surround ourselves with things we believe will make us happy. It could be a new car, new job, friends, love interest, or even food. But, because these things are tangible, they can be taken away. In the case of a love interest, they can withdraw their love without your permission.

God offers us His way of life and all that comes with it, which no living person can strip away from us. Even in the darkest times, His joy will fill us with peace.

Prayer Suggestion

Ask God to fill every area of your life with His true peace, love and joy.

GOD CREATED YOU FOR A PURPOSE

Proverbs 16: 1-4
"The plans of the heart belong to man,
But the answer of the tongue is from the Lord.
All the ways of a man are clean in his own sight,
But the Lord weighs the motives.
Commit your works to the Lord,
And your plans will be established.
The Lord has made everything for its own purpose,
Even the wicked for the day of evil."

In the passage above, it is clear that God has a plan or purpose for everyone. Even wicked people have a place in His grand plan. How much more, then, must there be a wonderful plan God has for you as a Christian? The ultimate purpose of everyone who walks with God is to bring our world and its people into a closer relationship with God. He longs to be reconciled with his creation, and each of us has a role to play in reconciling God and His people.

But that's a general idea – what about the specifics? What can *you* as one person do to fulfill your purpose? Pray for guidance and ask God to reveal His purpose for you. Take the time to evaluate your life and what the true desires of your heart is. If you could forget all obstacles, such as time and money, what is the one thing you long to do with your life? What is your passion? What are your true talents and gifts?

Guess what? God is the one who put those dreams in your heart and give you the gifts that are uniquely yours! If he has put a passion in your soul, it is because He wants you to use that passion to further His kingdom. If you have been blessed with a particular talent, it is because He desires that you use your talents in His name. Take the time to ask God how you can use your passions and gifts to glorify Him, and you will have found your true Purpose.

Prayer Suggestion

Lay your passions, gifts and talents before the Lord. Ask Him to consecrate them to His work and seek His guidance in using them to help others and establish God's kingdom.

GOD WANTS HIS VERY BEST FOR YOU

Psalms 1:1-3
"Blessed is the man
who does not walk in the counsel of the wicked
or stand in the way of sinners
or sit in the seat of mockers.
But his delight is in the law of the Lord,
And on His law he meditates day and night.
His is like a tree planted by streams of water,
Which yields its fruit in season
And whose leaf does not whither.
Whatever he does prospers."

The psalm above clearly shows that we will, as followers of God, thrive and prosper in ways that those who are wicked or willfully sinful won't. Some Christians are surprised by this psalm, believing that we are all called on to suffer for Christ's sake. It may be that some of us will have to suffer, but that isn't what God *wants* for us. He wants us to enjoy happiness and a good life resting in His Grace.

What stands between us and the very best that God wants for us isn't God, but this world. When we plant our hopes in the love of money, the actions of others or even ourselves, we have pulled up our roots and planted them away from those nourishing waters that help us thrive.

When we plant our dreams and desires in God's word so that they are nourished by His love and blessings, they can thrive, just like the tree in the first Psalm. God nourishes our lives with His love and care so that we are protected from harm and able to flourish in this world despite the problems surrounding us.

Remember today that God wants the very best for us and will provide it to anyone who lives according to His word and nourishes his soul with God's promises.

Prayer Suggestion

Thank God for his loving care for you and His gift of all the best that He has to offer. Ask Him to bless you with the best that He has for you, and devote your life to His word in thanks.

HOW DO YOU COPE WITH BAD NEWS?

Psalm 55:22
"Cast your cares upon the Lord
and He will sustain you;
He will never let the righteous fall.
But you, O God, will bring down the wicked
into the pit of corruption;
bloodthirsty and deceitful men
will not live out half their days.
But as for me, I trust in You."

The world is a fallen place, filled with sorrows of every kind. Sometimes we face a true tragedy, such as the death of a dear friend or loved one. We may also face stressful, sad situations such as the loss of a job, the ending of a precious relationship, foreclosure on a home or bad news from our doctor.

Does this mean God doesn't care? Not at all! In the Bible we learn that God actually watches over our destiny to such an extent that He is ready and waiting to sustain you and take you through any kind of suffering imaginable. He promises that the righteous will never fall, that your suffering is only momentary and will come to an end, while the wicked will not recover.

What a wonderful blessing to know that God will never let us receive bad news without also promising to sustain and strengthen us. Despite the worst the world can throw at us, He will never let you fall! If you can live like the writer of the Psalm, who admits to God, "I trust in You," you will always find the strength to triumph over whatever sorrows come your way.

The key is *trusting in God, not yourself,* to give you the strength and guidance you need to survive and move beyond bad news. If you can put Him in charge during the worst of times, you will have your reward in the better times ahead.

Prayer Suggestion

Lay at God's feet whatever bad news or sorrow is weighing on you. Let go of your need to control everything and simply trust fully in God to sustain you. Ask God to see and understand your sorrow and to give you the strength you need to move forward.

GOD CAN CREATE THE BEST FUTURE FOR YOU

> *Jeremiah 29:11-12*
> *"'For I know the plans I have for you,' declares the Lord, 'plans to prosper you and not to harm you, plans to give you hope and a future. Then you will call upon me, and I will listen to you. You will seek me and find me when you seek me with all your heart.' 'I will be found by you,' declares the Lord, 'and I will bring you back from captivity.'"*

We love to plan out our own lives and chart the course we think it should take, aiming for the kind of happiness and success we've always dreamed about. And we may seek advice and guidance from friends, family and co-workers, hoping that they can tell us the right choices to make and the right path to follow. We hope that these people want what is best for us, but even those who love us may be torn in their loyalties or mistaken in their advice. After all, they want what is best for themselves as well as you, and they certainly can't see the future!

But if you put your full faith in God's guidance, you will find the path to what will make you happiest and is best for you. God promises clearly that he *already has plans for us in place,* and we only have to call upon Him to find out what those plans are. God clearly sees the future and knows what is going to happen – no one else can know the future, so no one else can guide you as surely and honestly without steering you in the wrong direction.

God will reveal His plan to you if only you are willing to ask Him and truly listen. We may sometimes face hard times or detours, but God knows that these are necessary detours that we have to take in order to get us where we should be going. How wonderful that God clearly sees the future and can put us on the right path, knowing that no matter what happens along the way, we will end up at the best possible future for us as God's children.

Prayer Suggestion

Ask the Lord to grant you the patience and wisdom to turn to Him for guidance. Let Him know that You trust in His desire to give you the best possible future, and that You will slow down enough to listen to His guidance rather than the rush of the world around you.

PRAY FOR OTHERS

Galatians 6:10
"Therefore, whenever we have the opportunity, we should do good to everyone—especially to those in the family of faith."

Prayer is the most powerful thing that you can do for someone. Many think it is a passive act that we engage in when we don't know what else to do. On the contrary, our words have power and life when they reach God's ears.

Have you ever experienced the difference between praying first and praying when you are at the end of your rope? In one case you start and end the right way and in the other situation you find a measure of peace after being frazzled.

Going to God in prayer for someone in need opens the floodgates of Heaven. As a child of God, He listens attentively to your words. That person couldn't be in better hands than yours at that moment. You have turned their life over to God for His divine intervention. And, He will do just that.

But, there is more than one way to be in need. Even our enemies are in need. We don't often think of it that way because they are hurting us. The Bible says to pray for those who persecute and use you. It is not to bring the wrath of God down on them but the love of God.

Your sincere prayers at that time could change their lives forever. Like Saul, they could have a "Damascus road experience" and find salvation. That is a true testament to the power of your prayers in the lives of others. Instead of another lost soul, you will have gained a brother or sister in the faith.

Prayer Suggestion

Lord, help me to see that we all need you, even those who don't treat me well.

DIVINE ORDER

> **2 Chronicles 7:14**
> *"Then if my people who are called by my name will humble themselves and pray and seek my face and turn from their wicked ways, I will hear from heaven and will forgive their sins and restore their land."*

If you have ever taken a science class, then you have been introduced to order. In the universe, things happen at certain times and in certain ways. Some call it the "natural order of things." In God's realm, there is a divine order to things.

The verse above gives specific instructions as to how God's people would receive forgiveness for their wayward actions. Unless they consciously acknowledged their sin and decided to change, their pleas wouldn't be answered from Heaven.

It is like light and dark. Neither can exist in the same place at the same time. When you light a candle in the dark room, the darkness is pierced. That's part of that natural order again.

In the spiritual realm, asking God for forgiveness begins the process of lighting up the dark places inside of you. Since God can't exist in a dark place, one of them has to leave. If you are not ready to give your life to God wholeheartedly, then you have a big decision to make.

To receive God's promise, you have to do your part first. Whether it is giving up a sin or changing a behavior, God makes it clear what has to happen and in what order. To gain true freedom, you have to first fall in line with God's spiritual order.

Prayer Suggestion

You can't live two separate lives in one body. Follow God or follow the world.

God Has Something Else in Mind

Isaiah 55:11
"It is the same with my word.
I send it out, and it always produces fruit.
It will accomplish all I want it to, and it will
prosper everywhere I send it."

There is a line from a contemporary gospel song that says, "God's delay is not a denial." God always answers prayer. It is just that sometimes the answer is no.

As a kid, you never wanted to hear the word, "No." It always meant that you would leave empty handed. As adults, we feel the same way about that word. We have even equated that word with a lack of love.

God is nothing but love and can show only that. As a parent, you are called to often deny your children something that you know will hurt them. It is the same with God. The funny thing is that we know when we are asking for something that we really shouldn't have. It's just that we hope God will overlook that and give it to us anyway.

If we were granted everything that we wanted when we wanted it, how many of us would wind up in a mess? God sees the big picture. He wants us to have the best but that does require saying no to us.

Resist the urge to get mad at God during these times. Keep praying that He will give you the answer He wants and you need. He is the parent who always has your best interests at heart.

Prayer Suggestion

Let the same mind be in me that was in my Jesus. When my prayers line up with Your will, the answer will be "yes."

GOD IS BIGGER THAN YOUR PROBLEMS

> *Mark 4:35-40*
> *"...Jesus got up, rebuked the wind and said to the waves, 'Quiet! Be still!' Then the wind died down and it was completely calm.*
> *He said to the disciples, 'Why are you so afraid? Do you still have no faith?'*
> *They were terrified and asked each other, 'Who is this? Even the wind and the waves obey Him!'"*

Have you had days when you've wondered if God could really help you through the low points in your life? Perhaps sometimes you feel like the many problems you face are so many and so overwhelming that you can't imagine how He could find a solution for you.

In moments like these, when you may be facing an illness in the family, the loss of a job, a bitter divorce or a child who has gone down the wrong path in life, you need to see your problems as God sees them rather than looking at them through your own eyes. Although you may not be able to come up with an answer, God will lead you toward a solution and shelter you during times of trial.

It can be hard to remember that, but putting aside your own fears and sorrows and looking outward rather than in will put things in perspective. Take a walk and enjoy the beauty of God's creation. Think about how He keeps our world spinning safely on its axis and controls the sun, moon and stars. Remember the many miracles He has performed, even to controlling the storms! It's much more difficult to calm a raging storm than it is to lead you toward a resolution for work woes, parenting problems or even the loss of a job. Yet He loves us so much that no problem is too small for His loving kindness. We aren't insignificant to God – He is powerful enough to take on all of our cares and more!

Prayer Suggestion

Ask God to help you, reminding yourself that no problem is insignificant to our Lord, who commands the wind and rain.

BEING A SERVANT OF GOD IN TIMES OF TROUBLE CAN BE DIFFICULT

> ### Daniel 3:16-18
> *"...If we are thrown into the blazing furnace, the God we serve is able to save us from it, and He will rescue us from your hand, O King. But even if He does not, we want you to know, O King, that we will not serve your Gods or worship the image of gold you have set up."*

There are two things that are remarkable about the words above, spoken by Shadrach, Meschach and Abednego when threatened with a fearsome death by the King. First, they acknowledge that God *is able* to save them, not that he *will*. They go on to say that even if they aren't saved from the fire, they will not worship anyone but God.

Can Christians today live a life of such commitment? It certainly is a challenge at times – we may fear that if we talk too much about God we might lose our jobs, lose a friend or even lose our relationship with our family. The hard fact is that these things could happen – God *is able* to save us from such grief, but He doesn't guarantee that He will do so. We have to have enough faith that we can be God's servant no matter what the consequences – even if it means burning in a fiery furnace, losing a job or ending a friendship.

To find the courage to do these things, we have only to remember that the true reward is NOT the praise or success of this world, but eternal life in the next. Every time we act as God's witness on earth, we are furthering His kingdom, and eternal reward waits us in time. We may not be around to see whether our work in His name bears fruit, but God will know and remember. He will give us all that we need for now, and great rewards in the life everlasting if we find the courage to live the Christian life today even against all odds.

Prayer Suggestion

Ask God how you can be a witness in everything you do, then ask for the courage to follow through. Praise His power to save you, whether in this world or the next.

GOD DIRECT MY PATH

Psalm 119:105
"Your word is a lamp to my feet and a light for my path."

Oftentimes, God's will is a mystery. It can be frustrating, when we feel like we're left wondering what He wants us to do. Sometimes we feel like we're guessing, and then second-guessing ourselves. It is in these in-between times, when we're not sure where we're being led, that we must lean on faith the most.

This faith can be strengthened by reading the Bible. God's Word will direct our paths, even if it feels like nothing's happening. We might read the Bible ten days in a row and feel like we're not gleaning anything that can be applied to what's happening in our lives at that moment, but then on the eleventh day, we encounter a bombshell verse that makes everything clear.

That is one reason why it is so important to read the Bible prayerfully. We need to ask God to show us what He wants us to see in His word, to ask Him to guide us with His Scripture.

We also need to ask Him to let us know (We can request that He do it gently) when we've taken a wrong turn. Sometimes we misinterpret His direction, or we listen to our own voices instead of His. It is at these times, that we most need His guidance, but it is at these times that we might be the most resistant to accepting it.

Prayer Suggestion

"Dear God, Please direct my path in every way. Please show me Your will through Your Word and in my life. And if I am on the wrong path, or about to make a wrong turn, please show me the right way."

Chapter 5
EXPERIENCE GOD'S LOVE AND POWER FOR INSPIRED LIVING

What does it mean to live inspired? How would life be different if we walked around inspired all the time? Did you know that this is possible? Did you know that this is what God wants for us? Did you know that this is what God wants for *you*?

To be "inspired" means to be guided, uplifted, and motivated by divine influence. Sometimes we think of being inspired as going without sleep for days while madly painting masterpieces. And while this is certainly an example of being inspired, it is *only* an example.

Have you ever drifted off to sleep completely content with the world, with your life, with complete assurance that all of your loved ones would be safe through the night, and that you would wake up to a bright morning? That's right! You can even have inspired sleeping!

Have you ever been in a difficult situation, but seemingly miraculously, you had the right words to say, and you just somehow knew that everything was going to be okay? You can have these inspired moments all the time!

God wants us to be inspired every minute of every day. He gives us the Holy Spirit to live within us, to guide us, to uplift us, to motivate us. He gives us the Holy Bible to guide us, to uplift us, to motivate us. He wants us to experience His love and His peace every moment of every day!

Your life will never be perfect. People will still cut you off in traffic. Loved ones will still leave this earth, and you will miss them. You will still stub your toe and get hangnails. But when you are truly inspired, life doesn't have to be perfect. You have the peace of God. You know that you are loved as a precious child of God. You know that you have the Holy Spirit—the very power of God—living within you! Don't get caught up in the stresses of life! You have better things to do! You have an inspired life to live! So, what are you waiting for?

EXPERIENCING A GOD ENCOUNTER

Exodus 3:2
"There the angel of the LORD appeared to him in a blazing fire from the middle of a bush. Moses stared in amazement. Though the bush was engulfed in flames, it didn't burn up."

What is a God encounter? Is it like the burning bush or the Damascus road? Or, is it something different like Jesus talking with the woman at the well?

God comes to each of us in His own way. He only said that His sheep will know His voice and follow Him. Well, His "sheep" speak different languages.

On the Day of Pentecost, mentioned in the book of Acts, the Holy Spirit indwelled each believer in the Upper Room. When they went outside and spoke in tongues, each person who heard them received God's message in their own language. How amazing!

Maybe God speaks to you in that "still, small voice" in your mind, in your voice. You know it is Him because you KNOW Him. When your relationship has developed enough and you are in constant contact with Him, you can recognize when He speaks.

Or, He may make His presence known through someone else in your life. The route of communication depends on you and God. But, when you hear from Him it is like the sweetest music to your ears. The God of the universe is talking to you, in your language!

If we stay in tune with Him, we can probably recollect at least one God encounter we've had every day.

Prayer Suggestion

Read your Bible. Recognizing God helps us to "see" Him more clearly.

GOD IS ALWAYS CHEERING FOR YOU

Isaiah 49:15-16

"Can a mother forget the baby at her breast and have no compassion on the child she has born?
Though she may forget,
I will not forget you!
See, I have engraved you on the palms of my hands."

The bible verse says that God has "engraved you on the palms of His hands." That's a powerful image, very similar to a person tattooing the name of a loved one on his arm. Imagine that, God has a constant reminder of you before His eyes for eternity! Anyone who lovingly holds your name in the palm of His hand can't help but be the ultimate cheerleader. He loves you, wants what is best for you, and will always encourage you.

You may ask yourself how God could be your personal cheerleader, but if we accept God as our Heavenly Father, it is easy to understand how and why He would also cheer you on. Think of a proud, loving father watching their toddler take his first few, halting steps. That father is watching, silently encouraging the child and hoping that he or she will succeed. After those first steps are accomplished, the father praises the child and envelopes him or her in a loving embrace.

Our walk with the Lord is like that. We may stumble and fall the first few times, but God is watching us, cheering us on and ready to pick us up and hold us close when we fall. He glows with satisfaction when we do the right thing, and encourages us to do the right thing when we are unsure. Just like a parent on the sidelines cheering their child on toward victory, God is carefully watching you and cheering you on to be the best that you can be – because that is what He always wants for you.

Prayer Suggestion

Thank God for His constant support and the many ways He has encouraged you or cheered you on in your Christian walk. Ask Him to continue to cheer for you even as you cheer others on in their journey with Him.

GOD, SHOW ME HOW TO LOVE AGAIN

Proverbs 3:3-6
"Let love and faithfulness never leave you;
bind them around your neck,
write them on the tablet of your heart.
Then you will win favor and a good name
In the sight of God and man.

Trust in the Lord with all your heart
And lean not on the ways of your own
understanding;
In all your ways acknowledge Him,
And He will make your paths straight."

After the death of a relationship or the end of a marriage, you may feel hurt, angry and betrayed. We enter into loving relationships believing they will last forever, and then have our hearts mortally wounded by betrayal or loss of love. How do we learn to love again after that kind of loss?

You must, as God asks us to, put your trust and faith in God rather than man. Keep in mind that you are still a wonderful, beautiful creature of the Lord, worthy of love. Continue to love those around you and remain faithful to God. This can be hard to do when we are angry and want to find someone to blame or punish the person who hurt us, but this only prolongs our pain.

Instead, learn to let go of those feelings so that your own heart is healed and you can learn to love again. Be slow to anger and quick to forgive. The Lord desires our forgiveness of others even as He forgives us. It's a tall order when we feel betrayed, but if we don't forgive, our hearts soon turn to stone, an infertile field for the seeds of love. If we soften our hearts and open them to others, the seeds of a new love will find a place to take root and grow.

If you trust in God rather than trusting in your own ways, you will realize that you don't have to punish or be angry at the person who hurt you; you can leave all of the decisions about the other person's life in God's hand. Once you turn over your desire to hurt them and instead give them compassion, your heart will begin to heal. Once your heart begins to heal, you will be able to naturally learn to love again.

Prayer Suggestion

Let go of your desire to revenge and your anger toward the person who betrayed your love. Turn over that person and his troubles to God, praying for forgiveness and peace for both yourself *and* the person who hurt you. Ask God to soften your aching heart so that the seeds of love can be planted there.

OUTLAST EVERY STORM WITH GOD

Isaiah 40:31
"But those who hope in the Lord will renew their strength.
They will soar on wings like eagles; they will run and not grow weary, they will walk and not be faint."

There will be storms. The Bible tells us that God causes the sun to rise on the evil and the good. Not just the good. And He sends rain on the righteous and the unrighteous. Not just the unrighteous. Of course, this verse is not just talking about literal sunlight and rain, but about the metaphorical light and rain as well. We will have sadness. We will have afflictions. People with faith still have to struggle with life.

The difference is: People with faith don't have to go it alone. God wants us to lean on Him in difficult times. He calls us to glorify Him when the roads are freshly paved, *and* when they are full of potholes. Then the going gets tough, the faithful lean on God. That's the way He wants it to be.

He wants us to hope in Him, and it is this hope that will renew our strength, that will give us the power to soar like eagles, to run like champions, and to walk with courage and perseverance.

It's sometimes difficult to swallow, but the Bible even tells us to rejoice in the storm. Sounds almost silly to consider rejoicing when a tornado approaches our home, threatening to destroy everything we hold dear, but it is precisely in the face of such strong winds that we are called to rejoice, because it is these storms that force us to lean upon God. Every storm has an expiration date.

With God on our side, we can weather whatever storms come our way.

Prayer Suggestion

Dear God, Please help me to hope in You. Please renew my strength. Please remind me to lean on You in the face of life's storms.

GOD HAS WIRED US ALL SO DIFFERENTLY

1 Corinthians 12: 4-6

"There are different kinds of spiritual gifts, but the same Spirit is the source of them all. There are different kinds of service, but we serve the same Lord. God works in different ways, but it is the same God who does the work in all of us."

Have you ever been told that you are different? It may have hurt at first. The goal of every person seems to be conformity. No one wants to "stick out" in the crowd.

God challenges us to not conform ,but allow Him to transform us with His purpose. For wanting to being the same, people have taken their lives, committed crimes and denied associations. Look at Peter. He didn't want to be associated with Jesus so he denied knowing Him to the crowd.

God did not create us all to be the same. The apostle Paul compares believers to a giant body. The body has different parts that must work together so that the entire body can move. Without the feet you couldn't walk. Without the head, you couldn't do anything.

Further on in the chapter, Paul talks about the gifts that God gives to us through the Spirit. The main point here is that the Spirit decides who receives what gift. If God has taken such care to choose who you will be, who are you to deny that in the face of mankind?

It is an honor to be loved and used by God. The fact that such an awesome God can use us is monumental. Your contribution in this life is important to Him. When people peg you as different, just smile and tell God "thank you."

Prayer Suggestion

Ask God to show you who He wants you to be.

GOD SAYS YOU GOT WHAT IT TAKES

Philippians 4:12-13
"I know how to live on almost nothing or with everything. I have learned the secret of living in every situation, whether it is with a full stomach or empty, with plenty or little. For I can do everything through Christ, who gives me strength."

In life, you will have days that you feel unsure of yourself. It could be the fear of failure or even the fear of success. You don't know if you have what it takes to do the job before you. Because we are human beings, this kind of thought pattern creeps into our daily living for Christ.

Even when God gives us something to do, we quietly question His logic in our minds. But you are not the first. Moses did the same thing. He stuttered when He spoke and questioned God at the burning bush for choosing Him to lead Israel out of captivity in Egypt.

Gideon questioned God's choice when he was asked to fight the Midianites. He remarked that he was the least of his house in the smallest tribe of the twelve (Manasseh). That sounds like some of us.

It may be natural to doubt, but God comes prepared. He gives us one thing that makes all the difference – the Holy Spirit. He works from the outside in to prepare us for what God wants us to do. No matter what God places before you, you have what it takes to overcome the circumstances.

Prayer Suggestion

Take His strength as your own. Ask Him to protect your mind from negative thoughts that stop you from achieving His goals and reaping the bountiful blessings.

GOD WILL GIVE YOU INNER PEACE

St. John 14:27
"I am leaving you with a gift—peace of mind and heart. And the peace I give is a gift the world cannot give. So don't be troubled or afraid."

The gift that God left for us was the Comforter – the Holy Spirit. He reminds us of the things that God has told us in the past. He has a knack for bringing us these words when we need them most: in the stillness of the night, in the midst of turmoil, when everything seems to be against us.

Worry is the enemy of peace. It leads to physical and spiritual upheaval in our lives. Physically, worrying can lead to headaches, gastrointestinal distress and arguments. Spiritually, you begin to doubt what you know – that God is your supreme provider.

It was never His intention that His children should feel anything but protection and reassurance in Him. But, we often mistake the peace of the world as the peace He left us. You won't find true security in things or circumstances that are based on human sources. It can always be taken away: money, cars, homes, jobs and etcetera.

God's peace revolves around an unshakable knowledge that you are His and therefore have a purpose. No matter what you have done in the past, God will forgive you when you ask. He will lift you into His loving arms and set you back down on the right path with a new frame of mind. You'll adopt His value system and also His way of viewing yourself and others. And, when you forget, the Holy Spirit will be there to remind you of the truth.

Prayer Suggestion

I know that I am yours, God, but sometimes my humanness gets in the way. Remind me of my worth in You.

DO YOUR PART TO PROMOTE THE PEACE OF GOD

Matthew 5:38-47
"...You have heard it said, 'Love your neighbor and hate your enemy.' But I tell you, 'Love your enemies and pray for those who persecute you that you may be sons of your Father in heaven..."

Jesus asks us to forget about the Old Testament adage to love our friends and hate our enemies. Instead, we are asked to love our enemies. This can be a difficult thing to do even when we are surrounded by those we love. It isn't easy to love those who are cruel to us or who have hurt those we care about.

Sometimes it seems that even those close to us, the people we love the most, have turned into enemies. Perhaps you're fighting with your spouse or your child is being defiant; perhaps your boss has in some way betrayed all of the time, effort and hard work you've given him. This is when it is *most* important to love those we perceive as enemies, whether they are friends, family or strangers.

We don't get to choose our enemies, and we don't get to choose whom we will love. God has told us to love everyone, friend and foe alike. Try this week to remember the importance of loving others in spite of who or what they are. Reach out to them and show them love. It may change things, it may not. But the result isn't what counts – the act of loving them is what God seeks from us. That love for others is a reflection of our love of God and His Creation. Do your part today to promote His peace by loving all those you encounter.

Prayer Suggestion

Ask God to give you the grace to love others no matter what. If you are in a struggle with another person, forget about praying to get your own way and simply pray for God's love to touch both of you.

YOU CANNOT HIDE YOUR SINS FROM GOD

> **Proverbs 28:13**
> *"He who conceals his sins does not prosper, but whoever confesses and renounces them finds mercy."*

Have you done something that you know is wrong in God's eyes? Have you confessed your sin with a contrite heart, or are you avoiding the issue, hoping the problem will go away?

Toddlers often do this. They may take a cookie they weren't allowed to have, or push down a playmate. When we ask them if they did it, they look innocent and say, "No! Not me!" even when we saw them do it. As parents, we know that we can't let them get away with lying about what happened, because even if they deny it, they did something wrong and they must admit it and learn from their mistake. We may even say, "I saw you push your sister, but lying about it is wrong. I'd rather you tell me the truth even if you did something bad than lie to me."

Then why do we so often try to ignore our own sins? Perhaps we've fudged a bit on our tax return, or gossiped behind someone's back. Maybe we have cheated on our spouse or been unfair to our children. But whatever the sin, we cannot hide them from God. Like a watchful parent, He sees our sins even if we don't acknowledge them ourselves. But we need to confess them openly and honestly; only then will we learn from our mistakes and gain God's mercy and forgiveness. God asks us to confess so that we can move on – the burden of a 'hidden' sin is one we don't have to carry.

Prayer Suggestion

If you have been avoiding confession of your sins, don't wait another day. Lay all of them before God and ask for His mercy and forgiveness.

LEARN TO SPEAK AS GOD WANTS YOU TO SPEAK

> *Proverbs 23:15-16*
> *"My son, if your heart is wise,*
> *then my heart will be glad;*
> *my inmost being will rejoice*
> *when your lips speak what is right."*

Do you sometimes keep your mouth shut instead of speaking up because you are afraid others will judge you for what you say? Don't! The Lord gave us mouths so that we could praise Him and spread the word of His eternal love and forgiveness. Many times we think to ourselves that talking about God is a job best left to pastors or priests, people who have studied for years and can quote scripture easily.

But God asks each of us to "make a joyful noise." He doesn't care if we sing off-key, don't explain things well or stutter. In fact, even Moses had a speaking problem – he stuttered! Yet God commanded Moses to lead His people out of captivity. If God expected great words and leadership from Moses, how can we give Him any less?

The proverb doesn't say "think what is right." It says there will be rejoicing when *our lips SPEAK what is right.* Knowing God is only half of what is necessary to live a Christian life. We also have to shout it from the rooftops – or at least share the Good News with our friends, family, co-workers….even our enemies! So stop worrying about what the world thinks about what you have to say, and start thinking about what GOD wants you to say. Then speak, loud and clear!

Prayer Suggestion

Ask the Lord to give you the courage to speak what is right and share His words with those around you. Commit yourself to saying what people NEED to hear – the word of God – instead of what they want to hear.

NEVER UNDERESTIMATE AND LIMIT GOD

Ephesians 3:17-20
"And I pray that you, being rooted and established in love, may have power, together

> *with all the saints, to grasp how wide and long
> and high and deep is the love of Christ, and
> to know this love that surpasses knowledge—
> that you may be filled to the measure of all
> the fullness of God. Now to him who is able
> to do immeasurably more than all we ask or
> imagine, according to his power that is at work
> within us."*

Why do we try to put God into a box? God created all
the boxes in the universe! He's only going to fit into
one if He chooses to do so, and even then, that would
be some box! Yet we are constantly trying to squeeze
God into a shape of our choosing. Maybe we do this
because we are trying to understand something that
our minds cannot comprehend.

What we need to do instead is agree to not
understand. God's love surpasses knowledge. Our
limited knowledge, our limited intellect, is human.
We are not supposed to understand yet. And if we
accept that, then we can find comfort and joy in the
not knowing!

Once we accept God's love, we become rooted and
established in that holy love. Our job is to work
to understand the love, because the love surpasses
knowledge. If we suggest that something on earth
cannot happen, then we are not seeking to understand
how wide and long and high and deep the love of
Christ really is! Why would we want to limit our
God? Don't we want to be a part of something so
unfathomable, so mysterious, so divine? Once we
agree to not understand, we can enter into a love so

grand, it will fill us beyond the limits of ourselves, and spill out into the world, and into eternity.

Prayer Suggestion

"Dear Lord, Please help me to stop trying to impose my human limitations on You. I know that my knowledge cannot fully understand You. Please help me glorify your mystery."

PRAY BOLD PRAYERS

> *Philippians 4:6*
> *"Do not be anxious about anything, but in everything, by prayer and petition, with thanksgiving, present your requests to God."*

A friend of mine recently said to me, "How can I pray about me finding a job when there are thousands of people out there without jobs?" This line of thinking can be extended in many different directions. How can we pray for a new church roof when thousands of people are homeless? How can we pray for our children when there are thousands of starving orphans in Africa?

These questions can truly boggle our mind. That's why we need to rid our minds of these questions, and give them to God. We can pray about the church roof and about the homeless people because God instructs us, through the apostle Paul, to pray about *everything*.

We don't honestly know what is and isn't important to God. We don't yet know the full scope of His plan. By limiting our prayers, we are assuming that we do know God's mind.

God wants us to pray about everything, the large and the small. He wants us to lay it all on Him. This is one of the reasons I love to listen to children pray. They haven't yet learned to be presumptuous enough to suggest what God wants them to pray about. They just pray from their hearts. I've heard a little girl ask God to protect the shadows on her walls and a little boy pray for his beloved dog.

We can ask God to end wars. We can ask Him to cure cancer. We can ask Him for a new church roof. That is the beauty of the power of prayer. It is through Christ we are strong, and it should be through prayer that we are bold.

Prayer Suggestion

"Dear Lord, please help me to be honest with You and pray what's really on my heart."

Chapter 6
CONCLUSION - MADE FOR A PURPOSE

A re you feeling like this all sounds easy in theory but feeling it's not? Faith requires trust, courage and perseverance. How is it possible for us to be certain of God's promises?

And we know that in all things God works for the good of those who love him, who have been called according to his purpose (Romans 8:28)

These words tell us that no matter what experiences we go through God works for the good. It is no accident that there is only one you. You are unique, special and loved by God. God shaped and created you to find Him and to need Him.

When we place Jesus Christ at the center of our world we experience God's love and forgiveness. No matter what we go through, the peace sustains us. With God in our lives, Jesus is our best friend, pre-empting the later words of Irenaeus he promises us:-.

I have come that they may have life, and have it to the full. (John 10:10)

The freedom we experience in our relationship with God and the realization of His glorious and amazing promises gives us lasting joy and abiding peace.
Until we fill the God shaped vacuum we will never know the glory of God's amazing promises, we will never know life to the full as Jesus promised and we'll continue to fill the gap in our lives by other means.

Turning to Jesus and inviting Him into your life will release the abundance of God's grace and blessing upon you throughout eternity.

What greater gift is there than that?

Your life will make sense when you develop a personal relationship with God.

You were ***made by God*** and ***for God.***

Live *your* life according to God's Word.

Don't accept anything less !

Closing Prayer

FAITH FOR THE FUTURE

Heavenly Father,

Thank You for the Gift of Faith.

Thank You for loving, guiding, protecting and blessing me.

I trust You with my past, present and future. I choose to walk by faith and not by sight.

I seek Your wisdom and understanding each day. Order my steps, day by day.

Mold me into the person You want me to be.

I have complete faith and trust in You.

Thank You for being my Shepherd.

In Jesus Name. Amen

ABOUT THE AUTHOR

Robert Moment has a heart and love for people. Robert's life mission has been to reach God's people and offer hope , inspiration and support. As a spiritual life coach, personal growth strategist,speaker and author of several life-transforming books including *Christian Women: Blessed Wherever You Go* and *Faith: Living Your Life Fully and Freely Without Fear*, he uses his God-given skills to teach , challenge and inspire individuals to find and live their life's purpose.

Robert specializes in maximizing human potential for purpose, happiness and success. People need to be uplifted, healed and delivered! God has done all these things in his life. Robert wants God to be proud that he created him. He is passionate about empowering individuals to prosper in all areas of their lives and succeed.

Robert's advice:
Operate in the fullness of God's Plan for Your Life.

Experience Life-Changing Power...

Visit Robert's Christian websites for hope and inspiration:

www.HowCanIFindGod.net
www.ChristianInspirational.org

Contact Robert for Spiritual Life Coaching, Speaking and Workshop Opportunities at:

Email: Robert@ChristianInspirational.org

More Information
The following books are available for bulk sale :

Help Me Find God
Christian Women: Blessed Wherever You Go
Faith: Living Your Life Fully and Freely Without Fear
Emotional Healing

To inquire about pricing for twenty-five or more copies (sold at a substantial discount, non-returnable), please send an email message to:
Robert@ChristianInspirational.org

www.ingramcontent.com/pod-product-compliance
Lightning Source LLC
La Vergne TN
LVHW021351080426
835508LV00020B/2223